APALACHICOLA BAY

by M. Weber

CHERRY LAKE PUBLISHING • ANN ARBOR, MICHIGAN

Published in the United States of America by:

CHERRY LAKE PRESS

2395 South Huron Parkway, Suite 200, Ann Arbor, MI 48104
www.cherrylakepublishing.com

Reading Adviser: Marla Conn MS, Ed., Literacy specialist, Read-Ability, Inc.

Series Adviser: Amy Reese, Coordinator of Elementary Science; Howard County School
System, MD; President of Maryland Science Supervisors Association

Book Design: Book Buddy Media

Photo Credits: ©Mai Vu/Getty Images, background (pattern), ©John Wijsman/Shutterstock, cover (front top),
©Wikimedia, cover (bottom left), ©4kodiak/Getty Images, cover (bottom right), ©iStockphoto/Getty Images,
cover (lined paper), ©Rainer Lesniewski/Getty Images, cover (map), ©Pixabay, cover (red circle), ©Devanath/
Pixabay, (paperclips), ©louanapires/Pixabay, (paper texture), ©John_Wijsman/Getty Images, 1, ©Svetlana Foote/
Shutterstock, 3 (bottom left), ©4kodiak/Getty Images, 3 (bottom right), ©Larwin/Shutterstock, 4, ©Jake Osborne/
Shutterstock, 5, ©Rainer Lesniewski/Shutterstock, 6, ©Photo by warhorse./Getty Images, 7, ©Carolyn Davidson Hicks/
Shutterstock, 8, ©Crystal Eye Studio/Shutterstock, 9, ©Jacob Boomsma/Shutterstock, 10, ©richcarey/Getty Images,
11, ©James R.D. Scott/Getty Images, 13, ©larrybraunphotography.com/Getty Images, 14, ©RugliG/Getty Images, 15
(top), ©EddWestmacott/Getty Images, 15 (bottom), ©BrianLasenby/Getty Images, 16, ©hocus-focus/Getty Images, 17,
©lauradyoung/Getty Images, 18, ©feathercollector/Getty Images, 19, ©Melissa McMasters/Flickr, 20, ©Engbretson,
Eric/U.S. Fish and Wildlife Service/Wikimedia, 21, ©frantic00/Shutterstock, 22, ©Flickr, 23, ©kali9/Getty Images, 24,
©Ebyabe/Wikimedia, 25, ©helovi/Getty Images, 26, ©Jacob Boomsma/Shutterstock, 27, ©malerapaso/Getty Images,
28 (cup), ©subjug/Getty Images, 28 (paper), ©D E N N I S A X E R Photography/Getty Images, cover (back)

Library of Congress Cataloging-in-Publication Data has been filed and is available at catalog.loc.gov

Cherry Lake Publishing would like to acknowledge the work of the Partnership for 21st Century Learning, a
Network of Battelle for Kids. Please visit *http://www.battelleforkids.org/networks/p21* for more information.

Printed in the United States of America
Corporate Graphics

CONTENTS

CHAPTER 1

The Systems of Apalachicola Bay

The state of Florida has over 8,000 miles (12,875 kilometers) of coastline. Apalachicola Bay is part of that coastline. It is in the northwest corner of Florida. The bay covers about 214 square miles (554 square km). There are four islands that are part of the bay. St. George Island and Cape St. George Island are in the south of the bay. They are long and narrow. St. Vincent Island is in the west. Dog Island is to the east. The islands separate the bay from the Gulf of Mexico.

*The ANERR protects Apalachicola Bay and also provides education about the animals, birds, and plants that live in the bay.

The majority of the bay is in the Apalachicola National Estuarine Research Reserve (ANERR). The ANERR was created in 1979. Its purpose is to preserve natural resources in the Apalachicola area. The bay is also a United Nations Educational, Scientific, and Cultural Organization (UNESCO) World **Biosphere** Reserve. It is a protected area. It is protected to create a balanced relationship between people and nature.

Every natural system on Earth is made up of four parts, or spheres. In a bay, the **hydrosphere** is very important. It is made up of all the water in a system. Apalachicola Bay is an **estuary**. An estuary has both freshwater and saltwater. The freshwater in Apalachicola Bay comes from the Apalachicola River. The saltwater travels around the islands from the ocean. The water in the bay ranges from 56 to 80 degrees Fahrenheit (13 to 27 degrees Celsius).

The Apalachicola River is the largest river by water volume in Florida.

The air in the bay is part of the **atmosphere**. The air is **humid**. The average rainfall is 56 inches (142 centimeters) a year. This creates a warm climate. The average temperature is 68°F (20°C). However, average temperatures can be as high as 90°F (32°C) in the summer months. In the winter, average low temperatures can be as cool as 43°F (6°C).

The biosphere is made up of plant and animal life. Apalachicola Bay supports a wide diversity of wildlife. There are more than 1,000 species of plants found in and around the bay. Birds, mammals, and fish are common. The bay's **basin** is home to reptiles and amphibians. This includes more than 80 species of reptiles. It is the highest **density** of reptiles and amphibians living in one place in North America. Some animals live in the bay year-round. Other animals only spend part of the year in the estuary. Blue crabs can travel more than 300 miles (483 km) to **spawn** in the waters of the bay.

* The blue crab's scientific name is *Callinectes sapidus*, which means "savory beautiful swimmer."

The land around and beneath the water of the bay is part of the **geosphere**. This includes coastline and land around the Apalachicola River. In the estuary, the land is covered in oyster beds. Oyster beds are hard. They can resemble rocks. The sand is full of shells. The Apalachicola River brings mud into the bay. This covers the ground beneath the water.

CHAPTER 2

The Apalachicola Bay Watershed

The Apalachicola Bay watershed consists of the rivers and **tributaries** that feed into Apalachicola Bay. The Apalachicola River is over 100 miles (161 km) long. It is the largest river in Florida. It is the fifth-largest river that meets the Gulf of Mexico. Farther upstream it also forms part of the border between Florida and Georgia. The Chattahoochee and Flint Rivers flow into the Apalachicola River. The Apalachicola, Chattahoochee, and Flint Rivers make up the ACF River Basin, or the Apalachicola Basin. The basin covers an area up to about 20,000 square miles (51,800 sq km). The basin also stretches into the states of Georgia and Alabama.

* The forests around the Apalachicola River contain some of the oldest trees in the southern United States.

Watershed Diagram

The Apalachicola watershed touches three states before ending in the Gulf of Mexico. Its long route creates a beautiful environment from land to ocean.

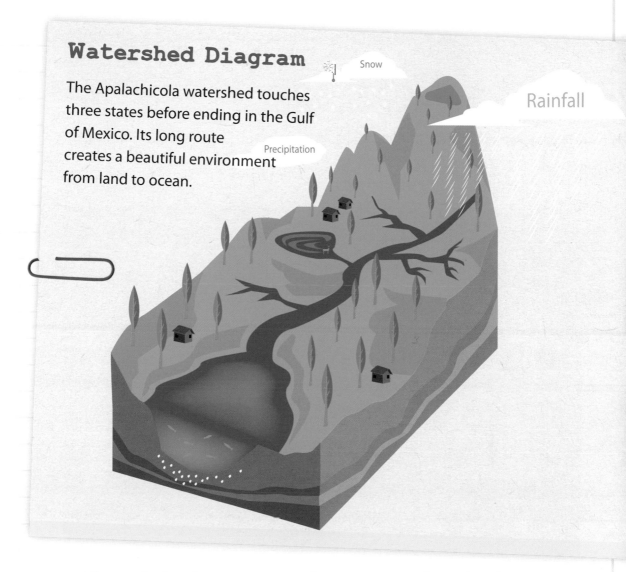

Snow

Rainfall

Precipitation

The Apalachicola River is one of many Outstanding Florida Waters, a list of special lakes, rivers, and other waters around the state. Bodies of water on the list receive special protection. The river is managed between the state and federal governments. The water quality is regulated to keep the river healthy. All activities that impact the river must be "clearly in the public interest." That means that anything that would harm wildlife or water quality is restricted.

The ACF River Basin covers many different habitats. There are forests and grass. The forests are home to many mammals and include Apalachicola National Forest. The basin also touches many cities. This includes big cities like Atlanta, Georgia. It also includes smaller cities like the town of Apalachicola, Florida.

* Fewer than 3,000 people live in the small town of Apalachicola.

The rivers meet the ocean in the estuary. There is rich diversity in the estuary. The mud the rivers bring into the bay is called **sediment**. Sediment can travel down the rivers from the mountains. It is made up of sand, clay, and silt. Silt is very fine sand or clay. This variety of sediment provides a rich environment in the bay. The bay supports environments such as **floodplain** wetlands and coastal uplands.

* There are about 72 known species of sea grass in the world.

One of the largest **contiguous** areas of sea grass in the United States is found near Apalachicola Bay. The sea grass beds are important to the health of the estuary. Juvenile fish rely on the sea grass beds in order to grow. The sea grass beds also keep waters clear. The beds keep the bottom of the bay stable.

CHAPTER 3

Plants and Animals of Apalachicola Bay

Apalachicola Bay is considered one of the most productive estuaries in North America. The area is very biologically diverse. Because the bay is protected, people are still able to enjoy seeing the wildlife and plants of Apalachicola Bay. The river basin is also home to many types of plants and animals. The Apalachicola River brings nutrients from the basin down into the bay. This helps wildlife flourish in the area.

* Black bears are the smallest bears found in North America. In addition to fish, black bears also eat berries and other plants.

* Manatees usually move slowly, swimming about 5 miles (8 km) per hour.

The bay has traditionally supplied nearly 90 percent of the oysters consumed in Florida. It also supplied around 10 percent of all oysters consumed in the country. The oyster fishery in the bay is the largest in Florida. Many people think of Apalachicola Bay when they think of oysters.

There are more than 50 species of mammals that live in Apalachicola Bay and the watershed. The Florida black bear lives near the water. Bears rely on fish from the river and bay for food. The West Indian manatee makes its home in the bay. It is currently listed as a threatened species. Manatees are sometimes called "sea cows" because they are large and gentle animals. They eat the sea grass that grows in the bay. In 1991, there were about 1,000 manatees in Florida. Today there are over 6,000. The manatee has been able to recover in the protected waters of Apalachicola Bay.

The bay is well known for its plant life. There are around 1,300 species of plants in the bay and watershed. There are also 127 species of plants that are considered rare. It is hard to find them outside of the bay. Tupelo swamps are popular places to visit in the bay. The tupelo tree is a tree that grows at the edge of water and land. The roots grow deep into the ground. The long trunk and branches often grow sideways across the surface of the water.

* Cypress trees are also found in tupelo forests. They can grow for over 1,000 years, though most today are less than 200 years old.

Honey Trees

Tupelo honey trees thrive in Apalachicola Bay. Bees use the trees to produce a honey that is very sweet. It can only be harvested for a short time in April and May. The honey never **crystallizes**, making it a unique kind of honey.

Fish are key to the health of the bay. There are around 130 species of fish in Apalachicola Bay and the Apalachicola River. This is more species of fish than any other river in Florida. Fishing is a popular activity for people visiting the bay. Common fish include trout and flounder. Between March and November, people also look for small sharks and bluefish.

* Many companies offer fishing tours in Apalachicola Bay for visitors who want to catch fish, such as flounder.

Birds also love the islands of Apalachicola Bay. **Shorebirds** are a common sight for those hoping to see birds on visits to St. George Island. There is even land set aside on St. George that is left undisturbed for birds. Birds that live in the bay all year include shorebirds such as black skimmers and American oystercatchers.

★ American oystercatchers search for food by wading in shallow water.

* Female loggerhead turtles will return to the beach they were born on to lay their own eggs.

Sea turtles are one of the oldest animal species on the planet. There are three species of turtles that are found in or near Apalachicola Bay. The most common is the loggerhead turtle. Loggerhead turtles can grow up to 275 pounds (125 kilograms). The loggerhead turtles come to the bay in order to nest and lay eggs. Like many animals, they benefit from the protections of the bay.

CHAPTER 4

Impact on Plants from Estuaries and Tributaries

Today the biggest threat to the health of the bay comes from outside the ANERR area. Damming on the Chattahoochee and Flint Rivers affects how much freshwater flows into the estuary. When there is less freshwater, the bay becomes saltier. This can make it hard for the animals and plants that live in the bay. The plants of the bay depend on a consistent level of saltwater and freshwater. In turn, animals depend on the plants for food.

*There are 13 dams built in different locations on the Chattahoochee River.

The endangered red-cockaded woodpecker lives in family groups made up of one breeding pair and up to four male offspring.

Apalachicola Bay is considered one of the five richest "biological hotspots" in the United States. This means it is home to many rare species. Many of these species are also endemic. Endemic means the species can only be found in a specific area. Biological hotspots can be fragile. The plants and animals have all developed together. Any disturbance can have a major impact on the health of the bay.

Invasive species are species of plants and animals that do not belong in a natural area. Humans bring the species into the bay. Some invasive species arrive attached to boats from other parts of the world. Some invasive plants come from local gardens.

The Apalachicola Regional Stewardship Alliance (ARSA) manages invasive species in the bay. Alligator weed is an aquatic plant. It is from South America. People believe it was brought to the United States on a ship. It grows best in a mix of freshwater and saltwater. Alligator weed can grow in dense layers. It crowds out native plants. However, it is unlikely that people can ever remove it entirely from the bay. Instead, ARSA tries to manage the growth. They remove large patches when it is reported.

Plants like alligator weed grow quickly, which is why they are hard to remove.

Animals and fish can also be invasive species. The flathead catfish is native to the Mississippi River. It was first seen in the bay and Flint River in the 1990s. It is a popular fish to catch. Popular sport fish are often introduced into new rivers. This allows more people to catch them. Flathead catfish can grow to be very large. They eat smaller fish. This threatens the habitat for native fish. By keeping populations of invasive species controlled, people are able to support native plants and animals.

* Catfish are named for the long whiskers on their face that resemble the whiskers of a cat.

CHAPTER 5

Humans and the Bay

Apalachicola Bay has been both harmed and protected by people. It is named for the native Apalachicola people. They were the first tribe to live in the area. The bay was used as a place to hunt and fish. People depended on the bay for food. In the 1920s, people cut down cypress and pine trees from the basin to sell for lumber. There were also many **canneries** that relied on fish from the bay.

* People in the United States eat 2.5 billion oysters every year.

Oyster farming has a long history in Apalachicola Bay, dating back to the early 1900s.

Throughout history, Apalachicola Bay has been a source of oysters. It is what made the bay famous. Families survived for generations by farming for oysters in the bay. There have been many threats to the oysters. An invasive species of snail called oyster drills was one. However, since 2010 the oysters have faced human-made threats. In 2010, an oil spill destroyed most of the oysters in the bay. The BP Deepwater Horizon oil spill happened on April 20, 2010, in the Gulf of Mexico. It is the largest oil spill in history. In 2013, the National Oceanic and Atmospheric Administration declared an environmental emergency. The oil spill had long-lasting impacts. The oyster beds are still recovering today.

The watershed of Apalachicola Bay is large and covers multiple states. This can sometimes make it difficult to manage. Pollution that enters any part of the watershed can travel to the bay. Pollution can come from many places. It can come from chemicals used on lawns. It can come from cars or trucks. Because there are many towns in the basin, many people rely on the rivers. Damming the river hundreds of miles away from the estuary will still impact all parts of the watershed. The Apalachicola River is one of the most endangered rivers in the country. It is **contaminated** by pollution. This creates an unstable situation for plants and animals that live in the basin.

* Although the oyster population has decreased, many people still visit the area in hopes of eating local oysters.

The bay has been harmed by people who live nearby. But people have also recognized the importance of the bay. The ANERR strives to limit human impact on the bay. The area it protects is large. It covers over 246,000 acres (99,553 hectares) of public lands. Public lands belong to all people. The ANERR has to work with many partners. The U. S. government, the state of Florida, and local governments need to cooperate. The ANERR also focuses on education and research. This helps people learn more about the bay. Learning about the bay can help protect it.

Torreya State Park borders the Apalachicola River. State parks are protected areas that everyone can enjoy.

It is important to protect the bay so people can enjoy it in the future. The bay is sometimes called the Forgotten Coast. While some activities are restricted, there are many ways to enjoy the bay. St. George Island is known for its beaches. People often visit to swim. They can also come to fish or look for sea turtles. Tourism is a resource for the bay. It can make sure the bay is enjoyed for years to come.

What Can YOU Do for the Bay?

One of the biggest threats to Apalachicola Bay is pollution from runoff. Runoff is water that mixes with oil, chemicals, and bacteria on the ground and then runs into rivers, streams, or directly into the bay. People can help protect Apalachicola Bay by not washing their cars in the streets. They can make sure their cars are not leaking harmful chemicals, such as oil or antifreeze. People can also use stones or pavers instead of  solid cement to build walkways and driveways. This allows water to drain into the soil to be filtered before it reaches the bay. People who want to help the bay can also join Apalachicola Riverkeeper, an organization that works with lawmakers and other organizations to protect the bay. Apalachicola Riverkeeper also hosts cleanups and educational events devoted to protecting the bay and its waters.

A 4-mile-long (6.4 km) bridge connects St. George Island to the mainland of Florida.

Imagine You Are a Loggerhead Sea Turtle

Materials:

* Sheets of paper

* A pen or pencil for writing

* Markers, crayons, or colored pencils for drawing

Steps:

1 With your teacher and classmates, research more about sea turtles. You can do this from this book, books in your classroom, or the school library.

2 After you have done a little bit more research, you can think about what it's like to be a sea turtle.

3 First, draw a sea turtle nest. Think about where it would be, what would be in it, and how the turtle would fit into the nest.

4 Second, use your imagination! Think about what it would be like to swim like a sea turtle. You can start a story about the life of a sea turtle.

5 Write as much as you'd like about the experience of being a sea turtle in Apalachicola Bay!

6 When your story and picture is finished, your teacher will help you put them together.

Questions:

1 Your teacher will let you share your story with a classmate or the whole class. What is special about your story?

2 What did you like about the stories you heard?

3 Does it sound fun or boring to be a sea turtle? Why or why not?

4 Does it sound easy or hard to be a sea turtle? Why or why not?

Glossary

atmosphere *(AT-muhs-feer)* part of the planet made of air

basin *(BAY-sin)* the area around a body of water that flows into it

biosphere *(BYE-oh-sfeer)* part of the planet made of living things

canneries *(CAN-ur-eez)* factories where food is sealed into cans

contaminated *(kuhn-TAM-in-ay-tihd)* made dirty as a result of harmful substances

contiguous *(kuhn-TIG-yoo-uhs)* an area that continues without interruption

crystallizes *(KRIHS-tuh-lyez-iz)* changes into a solid form

density *(DEN-sih-tee)* amount of space something takes up in relation to its mass

estuary *(EHS-choo-air-ee)* area where a river or tributary meets the ocean

floodplain *(FLUHD-playn)* the area around a river or body of water that can flood

geosphere *(JEE-oh-sfeer)* part of the planet made of solid ground

humid *(HYOO-mid)* moisture or dampness in the air

hydrosphere *(HYE-droh-sfeer)* part of the planet made of water

invasive species *(in-VAY-siv SPEE-sheez)* plants or animals that are not native to an area and cause harm to other species in that area

sediment *(SED-ih-ment)* stones or sand carried in water

spawn *(SPAHN)* to lay eggs in water

shorebirds *(SHOR-burdz)* birds that live near the shore or a river or ocean

tributaries *(TRIH-byu-tair-eez)* smaller rivers or streams that flow into larger rivers or lakes

For More Information

Books

Marsh, Laura. *National Geographic Readers: Turtles.* New York, NY: National Geographic, 2016.

Sill, Cathryn, and John Sill. *About Fish: A Guide for Children.* Atlanta, GA: Peachtree Publishing, 2017.

Witherington, Blair. *Florida's Living Beaches.* Sarasota, FL: Pineapple Press, 2017.

Websites

Apalachicola, Florida Facts for Kids
https://kids.kiddle.co/Apalachicola,_Florida
Learn facts about Apalachicola, Florida.

Fun Turtle Facts for Kids
http://www.sciencekids.co.nz/sciencefacts/animals/turtle.html
Read more about the life and habitats of turtles!

Critter Catalog: Shorebirds and Relatives
http://www.biokids.umich.edu/critters/Charadriiformes
Learn about many different species of shorebirds.

Index

About the Author

M. Weber loves to write for kids. She has written about cities, animals, and the world around us. She lives in Minnesota with her husband and son.